This Head of Security Wears High Heels

Rose Catalano

Toronto, Canada

4000 Steeles Avenue West #29
Vaughan, Ontario. L4L 4V9

Phone: 905-850-8517 Fax: 905-850-8513
Websites www.gemstarsecurity.ca and www.gemssecurity.ca

This book is written for women who are
considering breaking into the security business for themselves.
You will read about the headaches, the heartaches and the humour.
Rose Catalano tells it like it is.

ISBN 978-0-9940452-1-8 eBook

ISBN 978-0-9940452-0-1 paperback

Published by

Night Owl World Publishing

Alberta, Canada

www.nightowlworldpublishing.com

Dedication

I dedicate this book to all young women who aspire to take entrepreneurship to a new place.

I also dedicate it to my loyal staff who have stood by me through all the years in this business.

Rose Catalano

.

Acknowledgements

My first debt of gratitude goes to Rene Diamante for introducing me to the complexity of physical security systems. You made it possible for me, as the new entrant in the technological security market, to hold a position different from the *status quo*. You have been my tutor and my mentor and continue to give me your unwavering support. Thank you does not seem to be enough.

To Don Sebire (no longer with us), I will always cherish his foresight, encouragement and the perseverance that got me interested and involved in the security guard business.

His stories of his field experiences and his love for the industry will never be forgotten.

I say thank you to my son for being the #1 member of my fan club, and to him I owe my sense of purpose. David, it means so much to me that you believed in this concept and in my ability to deliver.

I am grateful to my husband for his continued support and for being my sounding board. Thank you for preparing excellent meals when the going gets hectic for me.

To my daughter, the external HR critic, I say thank you for putting your best foot forward and not shying away from our discussions as I challenged you on some requirements regarding labour structures/laws. You make an excellent adversary, and you are always ready to lend a helping hand.

I owe great thanks to my staff for their many years of dedication and loyalty. I value your enthusiasm and the steadfastness you show as we work together to achieve our goals. I say thank you, and I know that this would not have been possible without you. I also extend my heartfelt appreciation to all of you who gave me the opportunity to grow and gave my company a chance without reservations. I will always cherish your trust.

Finally, I extend many, many, thanks to Ann Jordan-Mills (writer/editor) for her support, guidance and enthusiasm in making this story come alive.

Table of Contents

Foreword

How has it been possible for Rose Catalano to thrive with grace and power in a man's world? Wherever you are located in the world, the Security Industry sees few women at the top, and this author has reached that pinnacle through determination and perseverance. She has developed her own strategies for success, unorthodox as they might sometimes be, and she has made them work.

In this book Rose paves the way for more women to join her at the top by telling, in her own inimitable style, the story of her uncommon choice of lifestyle and how she made it. She shows you a way: Rose's way.

For anyone who enjoys the extraordinary, whether or not you are planning your own company, this is a must read.

Prepare to be inspired!

From dealing with the personal problems of her mostly male staff, to challenging incompetent tax auditors and dishonest suppliers, Rose tells it like it is. Her stories will provoke laughter, and sometimes tears, as she outlines her philosophy and strategy, and builds her blueprint for you through a kaleidoscope of daily events.

Rose Catalano

If you are curious to find out how you, too, could grow your fledgling security business from a handful of employees to hundreds (and even if you are not) – then join Rose in this journey of courage and perseverance. She is a true pioneer in a lifestyle as unique as her story.

By Ann Jordan-Mills
Writer and Editor

Preface

A woman can make it in a man's business. I know, because I have spent twenty four years in such a business - the business of security. And I believe my success story will help any woman thinking about starting her own business.

It doesn't matter the kind of business you're interested in starting -- traditional or non-traditional. Or whether you want to stay small, or grow from two employees in a small office to hundreds as I have. You can chart your own path to success and fulfillment.

While my business is located in Canada, and each province has its own regulations, I believe that the same principles would apply anywhere. Moreover, my journey would have been similar wherever I had lived ... we all need to feel secure and protected in our daily lives. And, sad to say, as far as I can ascertain, I am one of very few women in the business, anywhere I look.

I invite you to join me as I share stories along my journey towards building a successful security business. You'll not only learn how to trim time off your own journey, but you will know how to recognize and avoid some of the common pitfalls that I blundered into.

I also invite you to enjoy some lighter moments with me. Various providers and others have uttered some very telling comments about me and my style of conducting business. You will find these words inside for your enjoyment. I have called them 'Words about Rose'.

I believe you'll find encouragement and enlightenment when you laugh (and maybe cry) with me, as you experience the roller coaster of emotions of being in business for yourself. I'm sharing it all, including the times I suffered doubt and despair and questioned my sanity in going into this business. But I also share the moments of joy and elation ... and there were many.

Now, I can't promise my book will make you successful; you know that. What I promise is that you'll be well-equipped for what to expect and how to deal with the many challenges you will face.

This book tells the story of how I got here and, more importantly, how I stay here - a woman in a man's world. For as long as I have been in this security business, I still need to continue proving myself to the men who are my competitors, and yet my equals, in the business.

I have written this book especially for women who are thinking about founding their own businesses. There are very many businesses that women can choose and in which they can enjoy success – both traditional and non-traditional - and this is one of those rare traditional ones that sees few women.

My business has grown and matured in the past 24 years. The Canadian Security Service is estimated to make up approximately 5 to 6 percent of the global market, which itself is estimated to be in excess of $2 trillion. Wherever you are in the world, you will always find a need for security, and see the signs of security in action.

Today, Gemstar and Gems Security are profitable organizations. We employ hundreds of full time staff and several floaters who fill in the part time and/or short term assignments. The company has expanded its horizons and we now have a good fleet of vehicles dedicated to servicing school boards, condominium complexes, building sites, and many more sites in the industrial and commercial sectors. We also keep in stock many kinds of emergency equipment, which could be needed at any time on any day.

So come along with me on my journey, appreciate the itinerary, and enjoy the anecdotes and stories that I tell. Never, in all my wildest dreams, could I have predicted what would happen when I began as a neophyte all those years ago.

Could you handle similar situations?   Think seriously about it. I have written this book to help you with your decision.

Rose Catalano

Introduction

Hurrying through the parking lot, and in through the back door of our offices, I stamped the snow from my boots. Immediately, I smelled the coffee brewing and felt the welcoming warmth of the building.

I wished Tony good morning, picked up my mug of the steaming, rich, brown, liquid from the front office and made my way through to the second floor. On the way, I received cheery good mornings from other staff, and was updated on the night's work. There were some issues to be solved, so I took the evening synopsis upstairs with me.

Despite the cold and snow, everyone seemed relaxed, which made me appreciate that they were glad to be there. I made my way up the stairs, greeting the upstairs staff on the way, and finally arrived at my office. Those few short minutes in the morning routine helped me to understand how my day would pan out and I began to plan ...

Rose Catalano

You see, I'm not the Executive Assistant. Nor am I the secretary.

No! I'm this company's boss!

I am often asked why I am in this industry, and my answer is always the same, "Why not?" Suppliers, customers, occasional hires, and others often comment, "You are the only woman I know who owns and operates a security company." They sound as if they cannot believe it ... but then I surprise them with some obscure fact of industry knowledge that they do not expect, and they reluctantly believe me.

Most of my employees are men, with a few female guards in the mix. This is a male-dominated business indeed!

I am a woman in a man's world.

The Story of Gems

This book is about how I founded and built my security company. **Gems Security Systems** (electronic systems) and **Gemstar Security Service** (guard service) are two discrete companies, but their stories overlap and they are one. I established my company in 1991 and, as a woman in this business, I have had plenty of adventures along the way.

If you have any business inclination at all, my hope is that you will read about my journey, laugh at some of the incidents I was called to deal with, and share my pride in my accomplishments. You may be familiar with how to open, run, and grow a business, but in the security business, there are a myriad of issues –many quite unexpected - that you will be called upon to deal with. Each section contains stories about the kinds of problems I encountered as I grew my business, and the approach I used to solve them.

Learn from these examples, be ready to address the kinds of issues I describe, and you are well on your way to knowing what you might face as you embark upon your venture. First and foremost, like many other businesses, we are a people company – because people are who we deal with. So if you are a people person, you will do well.

GEMS SECURITY SYSTEMS **Gems Security Systems** provides customized security systems and surveillance for property protection, such as access control, video surveillance, alarm monitoring, remote video monitoring, phone entry systems, and automatic door operators. We serve schools, warehouses, apartment blocks, shopping malls and more, in the Greater Toronto area and vicinity.

GEMSTAR Security Service **Gemstar Security Service** provides security protection against vandalism, theft, and physical aggression, and it maintains order, enforces regulations at public events, addresses personal safety concerns in the commercial, industrial, cultural establishments, and residential markets. Our officers are well-trained professionals who have been chosen for their skills in all areas of personal security.

4

Service Canada records show that since 2011 the number of security guard licenses has increased by approximately 40%, which translates to about 140,000 more individuals working in the industry. Ontario has the most licensed people at approximately 62,000, followed by Quebec and British Columbia at approximately 26,000 each.

Who am I anyway?

My name is Rose Catalano, and I do business in the Greater Toronto area and surrounding cities. My early childhood was very sheltered; I grew up on a farm in Italy with very traditional parents. My father was always the boss and the breadwinner, and my mother took care of our home, deferring to my father for all decisions. We immigrated to Canada from Italy when I was a very young girl and, while my father attempted to learn enough of the English language for his work in construction, we spoke very limited English at home. My mother worked in a factory until she suffered a heart attack at the age of 55. She did not need to speak English for her work, and so she was not much interested in improving her knowledge of the language.

My parents were old fashioned when it came to education and they did not see the necessity for girls to spend many years attending school, so I was never encouraged in my studies. However, ever since I was a child, I have been interested in numbers, and in High School I attained a perfect 100% score in my mathematics exam. While I was still in my teens, I saved my money and invested in some property in Arizona so, some years later, it was not a huge leap for me over to my own business.

(Here I am with my precious grandson, Dillon, when he was a few months old. He is the light of my life.)

I have two siblings; one could not realize his dream due to a work injury, and my youngest brother, through his own drive and ambition, is now Associate Psychiatrist-in-Chief at Toronto's Sick Children's Hospital. My parents do not have a clear understanding of his profession and therefore cannot share much interest in his work. As far as my own business is concerned, few of the family understand why I am here; but I am happy and I love the life I have chosen for myself.

A series of unexpected events headed me towards the security business, and that was the beginning of my unconventional life and my accomplishments in this unconventional business.

My mother still looks on in bewilderment and often reminds me that I take after my grandmother. I remember she was a spirited woman who made her own decisions and was very involved in many different activities during her lifetime.

My Introduction to Security

In 1988 an acquaintance, who was an electronics engineer, introduced me to security systems for the first time. He showed me how access control, video surveillance, alarms, and phone entry systems were installed and serviced in large facilities such as condominium complexes and office buildings. He also introduced me to two Canadian manufacturers of access control systems: Keyscan and Cansec, and he arranged a visit to the Cansec manufacturing site. This company manufactured access control products and there I saw a variety of sophisticated systems and devices.

When I discovered this technology, I was enthralled; I found it fascinating. And right there was where I created what would become a lifelong interest in this area of technology, and a thriving business.

I was hooked!

At that time, alarm systems were the popular security instrument, especially when the systems were monitored full time. An alarm system connected to a live monitoring station gave clients a sense of reassurance, though these systems ran into trouble when that live monitor (a person) was not physically present, or when the systems were only connected to a phone-answering service. However, right at this time in the development of security systems, access control and video surveillance systems were really evolving, even though these tools were still considered very new, and for the most part a novelty.

The visit to Cansec encouraged me towards more research, and I immediately jumped in and spent many weeks and months learning about this new technology. After much exploration of how the product all came together to provide electronic security for large institutions such as banks, schools, and shopping malls, I began to consider the possibility for other applications and it made sense to me that pursuing the security provider opportunity was a good move. The more details I learned about the capabilities of these products, the more I thought that this was a business I could, and would, embrace. Early on I could see that these Canadian-made designs had the ability to produce an excellent return for a business, and I came to realize I was choosing just the right time to venture in.

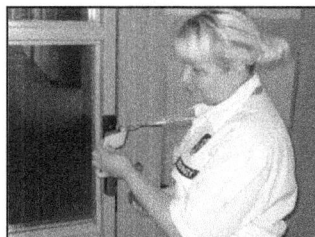

(Our guard using a prox card to unlock a door.)

Many of the security services and products were new at that time but, just like many other things we now consider necessities, I could see that they would become essential before too long. The products have become absolutely necessary to our lives, especially in our cold northern Canadian climate, and by adding such peripherals as proximity fobs, entry cards, remote transmitters, and so on, my business is complemented with a healthy residual income. Who in these days considers their garage door opener or their cell phone a luxury?
My instinct was right on the mark!

A Man's World

After my initial education and incessant inquiries about all aspects of the technology, I conducted a market study to determine the viability of this venture. What became immediately clear was that the industry was, and remains, mainly a masculine territory, and almost completely untapped by women.

13

It didn't take me long to realize at least part of the reason why ... the actual process of setting up the security systems involves a great deal of manual and physical labour, such as drilling through concrete and installing cables. Electrical Metallic Tubing (EMT conduit) and cable installation also requires some training in electronics and other technical areas and an ability to work with low voltage power. As well, the installers need to understand the structural features of a building as they are planning the routes of these conduits for installation. As the business owner, it was important for me to know about everything I was asking my employees to undertake and, where possible, that I had also gone through the same process, training, and experience.

Decision and Action Plan

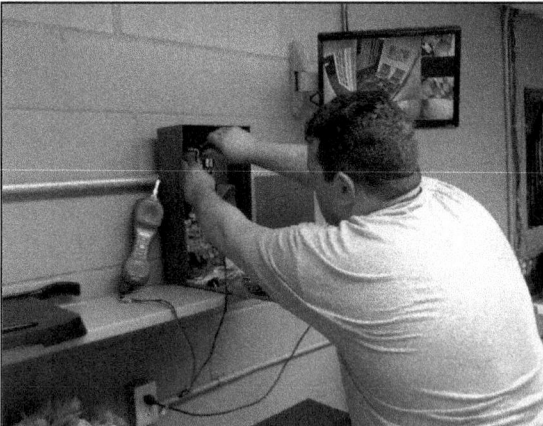

(An installer at work)

This aspect of the business would be no easy task for me, but I was determined to have my security system and service businesses, and I would not allow a lack of muscle power to stop me. I knew that the competition carried the advantage when it came to installations, as most of those contractors were themselves experienced installers performing the hard labour for each project. I thought through the issues and developed a specific and effective strategic plan while keeping in mind that this was all new to me.

I did, and still do, have one advantage in being a female in this industry, I have a woman's intuition. I believe that this awareness has served me well through the years and that my 'sixth sense' has been my radar, guiding me through the maze as I developed my business.

So I developed my plan, and I began to forge ahead with my vision.

Early Beginnings in Security

I knew before I even began that I would most definitely face many more challenges along the way but I had made my decision, and was prepared to take the risk, even if it meant that I would lose many nights of sleep in the process.

With a team of one installer, one sales representative, 600 square feet of rented office space, and me, the administration staff, I activated my initial plan. It took some time and a lot of stumbling to get going, but get going I did, and I have never looked back. It has definitely been an adventure!

Ignored by my colleagues

We inched our way gently into the security market and, as I began to seek out suppliers, most of them had no time for me. They would choose to discuss products with the sales representative only, who, of course, was male. The suppliers would drop into our office and talk to him as if I were not even there, and they would often invite the man out for lunch and leave me behind, not even having the courtesy to acknowledge my presence.

Security was, and still is, a man's space and at best, during those times, I would qualify only as the secretary or office receptionist in my own business! Today, I know first-hand that many men care about work place gender equality as much as we do, and for the sake of creating a more equal and better playing field, let us strive to be security professionals with aspiration to achieve a larger goal.

Aptitude and Attitude

To be a qualified contributor in this industry requires an aptitude for figures and a willingness to pursue constant learning and upgrading to keep up with the ever-changing electronic and technical worlds. Because of my early education and interests, these activities were perfect for me.

However, in addition to all the business and technical knowledge, there was another unseen element that many who were already in the industry did not seem to have grasped, and that was customer service. As well as superlative business knowledge, it is essential to treat customers seriously and courteously. Any business owner needs an empathy for customers' issues and without question should always work with them to solve their problems. I subscribe to the adage, "The customer is always right", and it is one that I prefer to use – at least until I am proven wrong, or until I find another solution that is a win-win for everyone. And no matter what approach the customer, or even my staff take, I personally maintain a voice of reason.

I must admit, though, that there are times when the litany of issues becomes a list of nagging problems and the voice of reason loses its foothold.

Moving Forward

After four years in the industry, I decided it was time for the sales representative and me to attend the annual Security Trade Show in New York. We wanted to learn about new products, meet new suppliers, and see what our competition was up to. Despite the financing difficulties, I was determined to increase the visibility of my business and become a viable contender in the Industry.

This Trade Show proved to be my turning point. Suddenly, the same supplier who had failed to acknowledge me since I had first opened the doors of my business, decided to recognize and accept me as one of his dealers. I also connected with an experienced distributor of video surveillance cameras, and for the next ten years this person became my mentor and my friend. Bill Brown was an icon in the security industry. He was open-minded and offered me continued support; he was my rock in my business.

Finally, I was beginning to feel secure.

Rose Catalano

That first New York Trade Show was a landmark for me, and today I still send key employees to attend trade shows and law enforcement conferences, most of which take place in the United States. Of course we are also present at the local conferences in the Toronto area.

Surround yourself with experts but make your own decisions

When you are new in the security business, or any other business for that matter, you should recognize your own strengths, and surround yourself with experts who excel in areas where you do not. So, since I don't have the skills of an accountant, a lawyer, an insurance broker, a vehicle mechanic, or an IT specialist, among others, I have accepted that professionals in those areas know better than I do. I seek and receive their knowledge, and I learn from them; they are my unsung heroes!

Following my own instincts – the Female Advantage

Although I am guided by other people's expertise and experiences, I ultimately use my own discretion and common sense when I make decisions. When I am uncomfortable with a professional's suggestions or recommendations, I have always found it is wise to follow my own instincts as long as I have a clear view of the possible outcome of the issue, or direction for my company. That, I believe, is a major advantage of being a woman in this industry. The addition of my intuition is what lifts me to a level above many of the others with whom I am in competition.

(The Gemstar Security crest)

For example, after two years of operation, my accountant suggested that I close Gemstar Security because he felt that the company was not, in his opinion, showing good enough bottom line results at that time. He felt that because the guard company was almost totally reliant on people, it was a drain on the company income, partly due to the guards' instability and lack of reliability. I maintained that even for a long-established corporation, this was the nature of the business and it could be overcome with volume.

I disagreed with my accountant's assessment, made my decision to stay, and continued to work hard at growing the company. I believed it had potential and the market was definitely in need of good and well-managed guard services, which I felt I could provide.

And it was!

Financial Issues

Though I disagreed with my accountant about closing down Gemstar Security, in truth I faced significant financial challenges in the first three to four years of operating my business.

When I opened up for business in 1991, it was difficult for a woman to borrow money for this and many other businesses. This experience was compounded not only by gender, but also by the type of industry. Security was not viewed (probably by men) as a business fitting a woman's lifestyle; she was considered not to have the time or flexibility to make it work.

Consequently, at the beginning, I was unable to establish a line of credit with the bank. This became a frustrating obstacle, and on many occasions I found the thought of entrepreneurship quite intimidating.

So for the first one and a half years, the company could only generate enough funds to cover the employees' wages and the fixed overhead expenses – there was no money left over to pay for my own time.

After about eighteen months, I was able to allocate a very small personal remuneration, and it took at least two to three years of continued hard work until I finally began taking home even a mediocre pay cheque. Financial recognition improved over time and then, after six full years of persevering in the industry, the banks actually began to invite me in to discuss financial assistance. How about that theory for playing it safe?

Where were they when I needed them? Their message was clear: show us that you are a survivor under strict financial limitations and we will slowly pry open the door for you. I became a part of a very odd statistic.

Voila, I had made progress!

Tax Issues

Banks and banking have not been the only financial issues I have dealt with in my business. When it came to taxation practices, I have also experienced some curious incidents during my company's growth, and lost time – and therefore profit – in the process.

All Auditors are not created equal

There is always the possibility that the representatives from the provincial or federal government agencies will pay you a visit in the course of your company's existence.

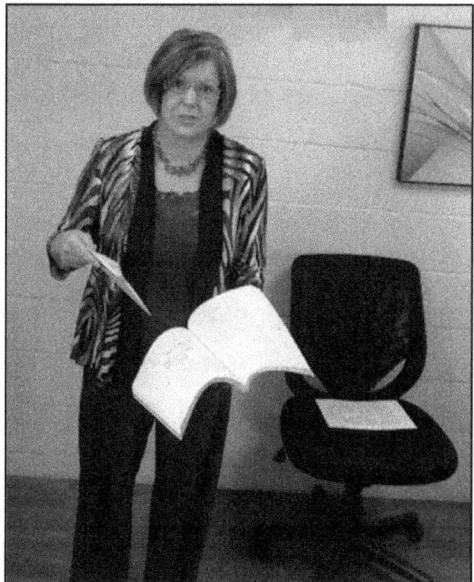

(I am reviewing Revenue Canada materials)

Audits can be called for a variety of reasons, for example, as the result of someone having an issue with you and falsely reporting you to the Canada Revenue Agency (CRA) just to make your life miserable. Or maybe simply a random selection. Either way, these auditors can sometimes be intrusive, misinformed and uncooperative.

#1. Hire knowledgeable support

I have had a few visits from Tax Auditors over the years and I have learned that there are some in that position who should not be there. I have also learned that I need to persevere when I believe that I am correct, and I know that the auditor is not.

～～～Story～～～

"A good friend of mine once explained that these representatives who come to assess the books of any company are simply government employees who get paid well to do their jobs. However, they cannot possibly have as good an understanding of your company procedures, your bookkeeping methods, your data storage, and your record keeping, as you do. Therefore, it should come as no surprise that *you* first need to teach *them* about your industry, then you show them how things get done, and then you repeat the process all over again hoping that their switch turns on and the information is actually registered.

In my experience, I have dealt with male and female representatives who carried a certain aura about them simply because they have the authority to pass judgement on your company's performance, according to how they see your application of the rules and regulations. They can fine you for the smallest infraction and they can add interest to this infraction fine, starting whenever they see fit. They can make it a nightmare.

These auditors are generalists and you need to make sure they have a good grasp of your industry and how the tax or labour regulations apply to your business. Therefore, I find it wise and advantageous to have an expert present who knows my system and is experienced in addressing the auditor's requests."

Rose's Insight: *Without an expert on hand to communicate with them and to file valid objections pertaining to issues that they mistakenly claim to have found, these auditors may demonstrate a total misconception of the facts, and can certainly cause undue harm to your company. The expert is also there to possibly save you from yourself. When you run the risk of telling these auditors what you really think, he/she* *is there to tell you to raise your right hand and cover your mouth with it.*

～～～End～～～

I once had an experience with a disgruntled employee filing a false claim and though it seems unbelievable, I had to deal with a provincial labour officer who could not conduct proper and accurate calculations because she kept showing up smelling of alcohol.

After HR and I spent a great deal of time correcting the auditor's first, second, and third spread sheet of incorrect calculations, I had no other choice but to hire an experienced labour lawyer to deal with this on-going ridiculous situation and hope that he would be successful in attaining a quick and proper resolution.

#2 Auditor under the influence

～～～Story～～～

"My assessment of this so-called auditor was that she was not fit to carry on with her agenda at any level and, if she were allowed to stay very long in our office, she would only succeed in aggravating my staff, and waste our time as well as our hard-earned dollars.

The lawyer's objective was to bring this woman's incompetence to her superior's attention. His goal was to avoid any further discourses, stop wasting valuable company time, and stop giving my staff a sense that our company was in the wrong.

While on her way out of our office one day, this auditor told my HR officer to make sure she came after me for any money that she deserved, and if she had to work any extra minutes on any given day, she was to make sure she got paid for that. Certainly, this odious woman made it quite clear to the HR employee that she had no respect for me or my company.

The appalling truth was that when my lawyer and the HR officer were able to meet with her superiors, even they could not understand or follow the methods she used for her calculations. They found the reports did not balance and the auditor could not explain where she got the amounts from. Once again, and funnily enough, she had joined the meeting under the influence of alcohol, and her supervisors were so embarrassed that they quickly adjourned the meeting.

After many months of chasing after this woman's seriously misrepresented work, and wasting much of my company's hard-earned dollars proving that the reports of this totally unqualified auditor were questionable at best, the claim was closed.

If it were in my power to do so, I would recommend to the Ministry that these sub-standard performers be sent back to school to learn more about the mathematical equations as they pertain to any business. Perhaps they missed these classes in their first run."

Rose's Insight*: The nasty reality is that when these auditors botch up, there is no law that says they must compensate you for your time and money spent. All you get to keep is your self-esteem and some sense of righteousness.*

～～～End～～～

#3 Service, Equipment, and Installation

I experienced yet another episode where the auditors knew extremely little about the difference between taxes for service, taxes on equipment and cable installation, and taxes on sales over the counter.

～～～Story～～～

"This auditor could not distinguish the difference between each scenario for tax implications. Having had some experience with the less than qualified government auditors, I once again resorted to bringing in Scott, an expert who specialized in provincial tax applications for the security industry.

If the process had not been so costly, Scott and I would have labeled it a tasteless joke. Watching the unqualified, operating in the unknown, and getting totally questionable results, was a frightening experience. Again, we went through the process of filing objections and held several meetings with upper Government management staff.

(Preparing the Power Point presentation with my Management Team.)

We used a PowerPoint presentation to explain the tax applications for security equipment *versus* for labour. We showed how we arrived at a certain amount of tax owing, and held many discussions about a number of projects. This seemed to make sense to the upper echelons and they made several revisions to the original assessment, including correcting misapplied payments, recognizing credits on returns and cancelled invoices, and processing credits on non-taxable items, etc. Unfortunately this was still nowhere close to being accurate."

Rose's Insight: *Once again I saw my company's profits being used to clear the mistakes created by the very people who should know the labour and tax laws as applied to security equipment installation and service companies like mine. I suppose there is a reason why labour and tax lawyers are in great demand.*

~~~ End ~~~

A sad situation

Shortly after my adventure with that tax auditor started, I learned that Carlos, a security contractor with whom I had been acquainted for a number of years, had gone through a similar scenario.

Unfortunately for him, he was just recovering from a serious car accident and was not in any position to deal with these issues effectively. His finances were low, as he had been off work for quite a while, and therefore he could not afford to hire a professional tax accountant. He was still in recovery from his accident and had very little energy to heal, let alone challenge anything that appeared out of place in the audit. This most inopportune timing of events cost this security contractor his company.

It had taken Carlos almost 18 years to build the company, and he was considering expansion before the accident that was followed by a visit from the tax auditor. Now Carlos sits depressed at home with little left in him to contribute to any industry.

As previous experience had taught me, I followed my instincts and, having the confidence that I had followed government regulation and standards, I once again took a stand. I have worked long and hard to make my company my Gem, and I was insulted and felt robbed when yet another unqualified person blindly put the gear in reverse and hoped for the best. I was not about to show any disrespect to this auditor, who actually told me to file an objection, but I was most definitely

Rose Catalano

not going to be intimidated by their collection department either.

So I did what had to be done! In the sorting out process, I made sure that the area Member of Provincial Parliament (MPP) and even the Minister of Finance were privy to what their staff's abilities consisted of, and how the efficient use of our tax dollars was playing out.

After five years of nerve-wracking struggles for all parties, the mission was over and we made our point. This really felt like a big victory for me. The accountant and I celebrated over lunch and then threw the old tax book in the garbage where it belonged. I felt that my stand had also avenged Carlos, the other security contractor, even though I did not personally know him or his accounting methods very well.

What Skills Do You Need to run a Successful Business?

As the owner of a small to medium sized company, you must wear many hats. You will be a mentor to many, as well as an innovator, a leader, a motivator, and sometimes, a disciplinarian.

The security industry is a service industry and you will not build a strong and trustful business by displaying arrogance or a know-it-all attitude when you encounter conflict. There are nasty and aggressive people in this industry whose first language appears to be profanity. They are trying to intimidate and bully you with their macho approach; so if that happens for you, simply refuse to descend to the same level! I certainly do.

To quote an old saying, "You catch more flies with honey than with vinegar". In other words, you should approach issues calmly and not try to bully your way through a problem. At the same time, however, I have found that there are certain situations where firmness and courage to face or stare down the issue (or maybe the person) is what we need. Whatever business you are in, you are going to experience daily and ongoing issues, so you need to face and put out the everyday fires, while at the same time trying to catch your breath from yesterday's blazes.

Here are some of the qualities that you need if you own a security business ... or any other business for that matter. Your goal is to model the behaviours I show below, so that your staff will follow your example. Mind you, just because you can show them the way, not all people know how to follow, and to expect perfect results from your staff is not realistic, nor is it even prudent.

- **Diplomacy**

When you are dealing with conflict, your key response should be diplomacy which, along with discretion and negotiation skills, will allow you to work through the issues. Use your mediation skills to re-establish lost communication, and find solutions to the issues at hand.

~~~Story~~~

"An office employee had problems urinating in the toilet bowl. His aim was so bad that other co-workers refused to use the men's washroom due to the constant urine smell and shoes sticking to the floor.

Because I was the only female working in an environment of men only, I found it a most difficult matter to address, but it had to be done, and there was no easy way around it. Even though most of the staff identified who the offender was, I gathered all the office staff together and made it a general address, because I found it extremely uncomfortable to discuss this issue one-on-one with the fellow concerned.

I chose to explain that everyone must use the facilities properly, leave the toilet seat clean and if they miss the toilet bowl, they must be sure to immediately clean the area. I emphasized how this situation posed a health hazard and was offensive to other co-workers. Of course *no one* was the responsible party, and blame was redirected to the dispatchers who work the evening/night shifts.

But ... my message was heard."

~~~End~~~

In another incident, an installer was uncomfortable with a clothing malfunction and made a wrong choice to deal with it.

~~~Story~~~

"Mid-way through the installation of an access control project, another installer working at an industrial site accidentally ripped his pants. He was uncomfortable explaining to the customer that he needed to be excused for a while so he could go home and change, so he simply left the site.

He left our office out of the loop as well, because he was embarrassed to advise the office that his uniform had no crotch, and that he would return to the site to complete and enable the system once he put on new pants.

Within half an hour of him being off-site, our office received a phone call from a very concerned customer asking us to send a different technician to get the project completed and all doors operational. The customer was unimpressed that this installer had played Houdini and disappeared without a word of warning to anyone.

Once all parties were made aware of the incident and the installer returned to the site, it was business as usual and the system was initialized without difficulty, but we found out that some people do not handle a ripped crotch very well."

Rose's Insight: *You or your HR officer must use diplomacy when bringing sensitive issues to your employees' attention. When I come across an issue that is uncomfortable for my management staff to deal with, I take ownership and deal with it – even though it might be difficult for me also.*

~~~End~~~

- **Quick thinking and a positive attitude**

Some issues need immediate action and decision, and excellent training ensures that guards respond speedily and appropriately, wherever they happen to be at the time of the emergency.

~~~Story~~~

"While he was on his way home, a young man was stabbed at one of the sites where we provide guard services. If it were not for the quick response of the two guards on site, with the back-up of the support staff, the victim would not have survived due to excessive blood loss.

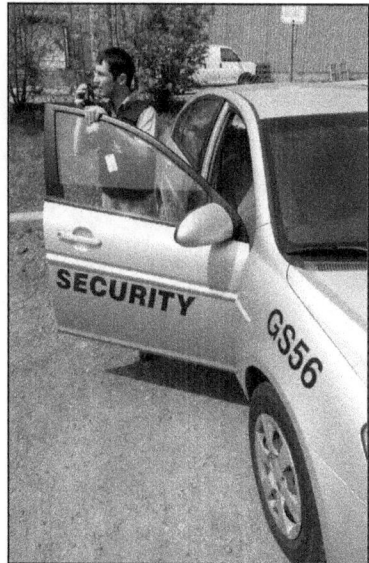

SECURITY GS56

(Responding on the job.)

Our security guards followed procedures by the book: the building was placed on lock-down, the police were called, and one guard attended to the wounded young man until the paramedics took over. The other guard collected pertinent information about the offenders and kept inquisitive spectators away from the scene."

Rose's Insight: *Thanks to good training and a quick response, this event turned out positively, when it could so easily have been tragic.*

~~~End~~~

- **Time management skills**

(Award from WorldWide Who's Who")

It is essential that you manage your time effectively and make the most of your workday – however long it might be. Your staff will learn from your modeling, and themselves practice effective and honest time management. Aside from managing the everyday administration, and the issues that invariably crop up at any time of the day or night, every action you take must be dedicated to growing your business. If you do not manage your time well, neither will your staff.

I believe that my excellent time management skills contributed to the honour of an invitation to be part of 'WorldWide Who's Who', and I received this award, with the following commendation:

"It is with great pleasure that we welcome you to our prestigious roster of Top Female Executives, Professionals and Entrepreneurs. We feel that your experience and professional dedication make you truly deserving of this honor.

Your profile on the Top Female website will highlight your distinctions and endeavours, and serve as an excellent way for others to learn more about you. We are excited to highlight you among other notable women, and commend you for your achievements."

Story

"My company's growth began to require more installers so that we could keep up with the projects that were coming in, so I hired a very dear person who had recently left his previous job to search for better opportunities. I had known this person for quite some time and believed him to be a hard working individual, though not a business man. My plan was to eventually designate him as the head installer/supervisor.

At first, I felt comfortable, believing this new hire would participate in actual installation and maintain my efficiency in the field. All went reasonably well and as planned - to begin with. He became fairly competent in the security field and always made himself available for extra hours to ensure the projects were completed on time.

Soon, however, I began to suspect that all was not quite right. My suspicions were confirmed, and supported by reports from other staff members. This fellow was habitually embellishing his actual working hours and travel expenses, and he was soliciting company business for himself by offering customers a discounted rate.

Then I found out that he was trying to entice the main staff to leave my company and join him for what he said would be a much better future.

It was very hard to believe that this man, who had confidently spent time in my office to discuss project progress, had been using me as a disposable tool to teach him the intricacies of the industry, while planning to pull the rug from under my feet. Or so he thought.

To his dismay, all his devious efforts and delusional hopes failed him miserably, and none of the staff followed him to his promised greener pastures. This was a nasty outcome to his corrosive plan."

Rose's Insight: *Like many business hopefuls who overestimate their capabilities, this individual mistook his position of trust and authority for business savvy, and he did not succeed. Honesty really was in short supply with this man!*

~~~End~~~

- **Resilience**

There are temporary setbacks in every business, as there are in other areas of our lives. Make sure you identify them as short term, and don't let them get the better of you, so that you can rebound quickly. Always try to be one step ahead of everyone else, particularly some builders you encounter who are not always 100% honest.

~~~Story~~~

""Enjoy the summer and go get your hair done instead of chasing us for the money you will never receive!" Those were the words of a customer's project manager who had stopped paying our bills and informing me that I would not get any more money from them. I thanked him for his suggestion and

told him to communicate anything further through his lawyer.
I said that I looked forward to seeing him in court.

Gemstar Security was providing security guards for a new
commercial site under construction in the downtown area.
The service was provided as specified by the customer, and
our staff worked well with other trades on site ... until the
project was nearing completion and regular payments began
to slow down. That was when we stopped providing service
and began collection activity. A meeting with a court
mediator was set, and then I began to get these phone calls
from the customer's project manager saying that we would
not get a penny from them.

When we had our day in court, three representatives from the
construction company showed up and began to speak loudly
amongst themselves, ensuring my lawyer and I could hear
them. We heard comments such as, "Women look sexy and
attractive, but they have no idea what it is like to wear hard
hats and safety boots on a construction site." And, "Women
don't understand the difference between a blue door and a
green door." They also declared that, "It is a waste of our time
to be called to court for this nonsense when we have real
projects to attend to." These men were doing their best to

create an atmosphere of great discomfort for me in front of the judge.

They were trying to say that services had not been provided. However, I explained to the judge how our shift reports contain details of actual activities and how mobile supervisors on duty monitor after hours situations.

The judge eventually ruled in our favour that services had been rendered and the customer had to honour their financial obligation. The judge further reminded them that if they were really unhappy with our work, they should have cancelled the service; however, they would still have been responsible for the costs incurred up to the day of cancellation."

Rose's Insight: *A stifling attitude such as this, is a sign of hunger and need for real training in business ethics.*

Such serious lack of objective business principles is a strong indicator that leadership alignment is required. Perhaps his organization does not possess any communication manuals.

End

A similar situation also happened on another occasion.

~~Story~~

(Installer at work)

"I visited a new construction site where we were diligently working on the implementation of perimeter alarms, video surveillance and card access systems, and I had an opportunity to meet with other contractors, the electrician and carpet installer. In conversation, I learned that payments were not being released to them, and they were receiving constant excuses and extensive delays from the builder.

Shortly afterwards, I was informed by my staff that the carpet installer had walked off the job. His company was owed a substantial amount of money and all he heard from the builder was, "Your money is safe with me". This installer was a lone operator, and he had a small operating line of credit, which by now was totally immersed in this project. Because he did not have the means to fight the builder, his company was now defunct. As weeks passed, our own receivables began to lag behind with this builder. Our red flags went up and after becoming familiar with his payment practices, I did not hesitate to commence collection activity.

After many, many, phone calls went unanswered, I twice went to visit the project manager with a Collection Officer, and finally got the payment that was due to us, with the exception of an arbitrary deduction of $500. Obviously this builder knew that I understood the rules of their business math and that I would quickly accept and deposit the cheque as full and final payment. Further collection activity on such an amount would be fruitless and counterproductive at this point. They boldly demonstrated that they were easily able to short-pay any contactor and not be the least bit concerned about it. They were the pariahs of our industry!

But, happily, I tabled the last word. Once their cheque had cleared the bank, I sent the project manager and their accounting department a registered letter advising them that due to a long outstanding $500 balance on their account, the equipment and labour warranty was now null and void. Needless to say, we never again bid on, or participated in, any other projects for this company."

Rose's Insight: *Being intuitive and well-informed is the key to building your company's status or success. When a situation like this happens, do not despair, use action before reaction, otherwise you may be a penny short and a day late.*

$\sim\sim\sim$ End $\sim\sim\sim$

- **Ability to Prioritize**

Make sure that you prioritize the activities in your day and, as in all busy lives, relegate your more minor issues to the bottom of your daily To-Do list – or delegate them. You must deal with the most important issues first.

~~~Story~~~

"Gems Security was awarded the alarms, access control, and video surveillance projects for a new commercial plaza being built in the north part of the city. Installation commenced as scheduled and the first payment was received as agreed.

After twenty alarm systems were installed in twenty stores, some DSC (Digital Security Controls) panels started to vanish, and equipment (including ladders and rolls of wire), stored in a locked room, also disappeared.

I brought this to the project manager's attention but he shrugged me off, saying that my claim could not possibly be true; perhaps I was confused about the equipment we had on site. He told me he had not heard of any other contractor with complaints about missing parts, tools, or equipment.

(Inspecting the locked storage room.)

This started to sound suspicious to me, so I immediately decided to visit my installers on site to see for myself where this so-called locked room was located, and perhaps I would have an opportunity for a dialogue with the other contractors.

That morning as I approached the premises, the construction supervisor instructed me to leave the site because I did not have the proper attire to enter a building under construction, i.e. a hard hat, a safety vest, and safety boots. I returned later that day with my sales manager and, surprisingly, had no problem accessing the site. As planned, we had the opportunity to speak to other contractors.

After gathering the information on this operation, my sales manager and I located the project manager and asserted our position. We clearly explained that if these practices were allowed to continue we would contact our insurance adjuster, who in turn would want to talk to his insurance company, and there would be a distinct possibility of an on-site investigation.

Rose Catalano

The project manager promptly made other arrangements for storing our equipment and the disappearance of the control panels and other equipment ceased."

Rose's Insight: *Without delay, I had let them know I was aware of the situation, and immediate affirmative action stopped the thefts. The element of surprise can sometimes trigger the brain circuitry of some of these project managers to actually process the information correctly.*

~~~End~~~

- **Delegation**

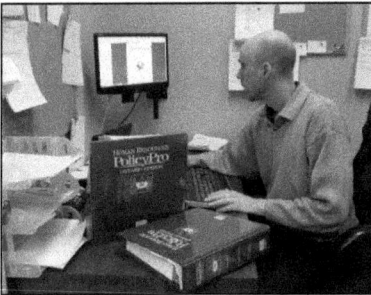

(Human Resources Manager updates all manuals)

Your primary role is to grow your business, so do not take on yourself what others can do for you. Make sure you know what roles you will delegate to your office staff. Then do it!

Your team must certainly contain a well-trained, knowledgeable Human Resources (HR) Manager, who oversees the screening process for recruiting new employees, is current with labour laws that relate to this industry, addresses confidentiality issues, ensures all Health and Safety manuals are in place and is capable of addressing employee concerns of any kind.

When your Human Resources Manager is screening for new employees, he or she must be well trained and knowledgeable about current labour laws, as well as Freedom of Information and Protection of Privacy (FOIP) laws. Both of these policies have rules applicable federally (Canada-wide), and in your own provinces – in our case, Ontario. FOIP and the requirement for confidentiality, particularly, are very strict and HR must practice the guidelines stringently.

FOIP rules must apply to employees, even at the interview stage. As well, our HR Manager must also maintain the Health and Safety manuals, and make sure they are current and up to date, as he is often called upon to address employee concerns in many different areas. In the past, this role was almost considered a phantom function typically performed by the individual who was overseeing payroll and other administrative duties.

Today, all this has changed and more and more organizations have become reliant on these experts' insight on management regulations, financial sustainability and cultural understanding.

- **Respect**

As the owner of the company you need to show respect to every person you deal with, from your largest customer to your part-time employee who fills in for you. When you show respect, you are modelling that quality for all to see and, in the same way as diplomacy works to solve problems, so does respect.

~~~ Story ~~~

"We hired an older gentleman to work as a dispatcher. We were prepared to allow extra training time as this position requires computer knowledge, radio etiquette, and most of all they must be able to multi-task. This new hire tried so hard to learn every aspect of the job that he actually kept confusing himself and, as a result, he mixed up the forms and details of alarm responses.

He kept reminding us that he was older and maybe not good enough or competent to learn new things. We assured him that we felt he was quite capable and to cut himself some slack, and we assigned different people to train him in the hope that someone would discover his learning style. For over a month we did not give up on him, and he became an excellent dispatcher and a most devoted employee."

Rose's Insight: *Respect for this man, as well as patience and faith in his capabilities, gave him time to build self-assurance and to learn to do his job well. He moved from being unsure and inefficient, to showing confidence, performing well, and becoming an exemplary employee.*

∽∽∼End∼∿∽

Everybody has something to say about Rose

~~~Competitor~~~

From a competitor: Over a lunch meeting, we discussed and agreed not to purposely pursue each other's accounts. Each respecting the other's turf seemed reasonable for both parties.

His observation was, "I just enjoyed lunch with an astute and tough competitor!"

~~~End~~~

~~~Colleague~~~

From a colleague who runs a mechanic shop in our area: "When my receivables get dusty, and revenue is scarce, I stop in to see and confide in Rose. She always makes things look so easy."

~~~End~~~

Rose Catalano

~~~Supplier~~~

From a young man at the order desk of one of our suppliers: "When Gems' staff places an order, we take it seriously; but when Rose calls, we're in the air before she says jump."

~~~End~~~

~~~Sales Staff~~~

From my sales staff: "The banner that I carry at our monthly meetings emphasizes strategy and instinct on a large scale. This seems to have had some positive results. At one point, one of the sales reps said that he was going to nickname me *The Mob Mom*, or *The Thinking Merchant*."

~~~End~~~

My Quick Business Philosophy

The A B C and 1 2 3 of my business philosophy is this:

Always

Begin your day with

Caution and Confidence

1. What needs to be done by tomorrow, should have been completed yesterday.

2. Welcome constructive criticism and adjust your ways if necessary.

3. Know and understand your competition.

It is essential to establish a strong base for your operation – especially if you are a female owner/operator in an industry that is mainly male-oriented. You *must* be well organized, have a strong sense of where you are going and most of all, believe in what you already know, and what you have learned.

(With three of my staff charting out new targets of opportunities in our area of service.)

Management Team

In order to run a growing company, it was essential that I build a strong team from the beginning. An investment of time and effort is the key that builds an inner team of people who understand your *modus operandi* and can work independently to deliver your requirements without too much supervision.

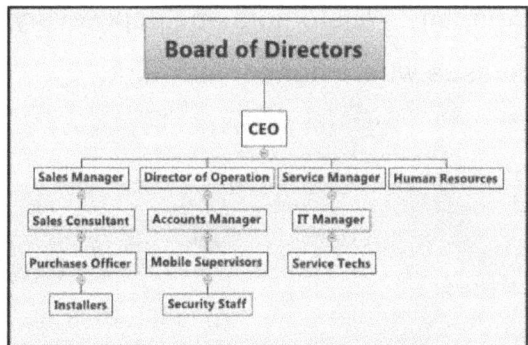

Sales, service, scheduling, installations, field personnel, and human resources, are the front line employees dedicated to firmly steering my ship and maintaining its true course away from troubled waters. At the beginning, I required a competent management team to handle all these departments through their growth, and now I need them to solidify and sustain our growth, which you can see in our organizational chart.

Communication with staff

Since I founded my business, I have made it my responsibility to keep the supervisory and management teams appraised of any new development or any change in company direction. Good communication is essential when you are relying on a designated team to manage your employees and your operation. The management team members are then empowered to disseminate this information to all the remaining employees under their supervision.

It is my responsibility to look-out for my staff and my company's customers and apply every available resource to foresee where danger may lurk.

.

Field Support Staff

High Level Delegation.

It was the initial ambition of my son, Dave, to be a police officer. He joined my company over thirteen years ago with the short-term intention of gaining some initial training and then moving to the police service. Since then, he has worked as concierge, patrol guard, dispatcher, scheduling officer, alarm response officer, and mobile supervisor. He is now a liaison for field supervisors and customer relations. Establishing top qualified field help is of primary importance.

Because he has experienced all of these roles in the company he is a vital link and source of support for the officers who frequently require assistance when they face all kinds of unprecedented encounters or situations such as break-ins, police attendance, arrests, parking enforcement, inebriated tenants, and so on.

Trusting my Delegation

Dave has been, and is, my voice in the field. He knows my directives and connects well with the field staff at all levels.

His position requires around the clock availability and a clear knowledge of field requirements, procedures, and subject de-escalation.

(Dave multitasking communications)

He often reminds me that throughout his years with Gemstar Security, he has learned to understand and value the effects of this industry's merry-go-round set of rules, while at the same time applying diplomacy with co-workers, superiors, and customers alike. Practicing and enforcing such policies is vital to the success of any security company, and I must have a trusted representative in my place.

Trust is an invaluable asset.

Communications with Dispatch

It is important to set up a fully equipped dispatch center that is manned 24 hours a day by properly trained operators. These people have *'dispatcher hearing' and they understand and respond immediately when someone is in need of assistance. These people have telephonic and radio access to mobile staff and emergency service technicians, and they are chosen because they excel in speedy radio responses to emergencies.

('dispatcher hearing' means that those staff easily hear and understand the incoming radio messages. To the untrained ear, the two-way radio communication may lack some transmission clarity, thus causing possible delays in receiving the intended message, and consequently exposing the person at the other end to potential harm.)*

(Dispatcher on the job)

I believe the service industry cannot condone taking short cuts in the interest of a dollar, and without a proper operational set-up, you invite the risk that your employees could be harmed and your customer could initiate legal proceedings.

Unlike some businesses who during off-hours can only be contacted *via* cell phone, I am not a believer or supporter of operating a full time service company without the ability to communicate with a live dispatcher 24/7. So far it has worked out well, and we feel secure, knowing that we are keeping watch when the city is sleeping.

Knife attack

~~~Story~~~

"We need to assign appropriate and skilful staff to extra-challenging sites. Marian, a well-trained and capable guard, was doing his exterior patrols of two sites when he was attacked by an angry, intoxicated, male with a knife as this guard was trying to remove him from the site. Marian is an expert in self-defence techniques, and luckily he suffered no injuries. Also his quick action to alert our dispatch centre ensured fast police presence and immediate officer support for him."

Rose's Insight: *We should get to know the individual strengths of our staff well in order to place them where their skills will be used to the best advantage.*

This will give you, the boss, peace of mind without needing to take sleeping pills.

~~~End~~~

Gems Security Systems Technical Staff

(A Gems Security Systems technician checking his equipment before he leaves on a call.)

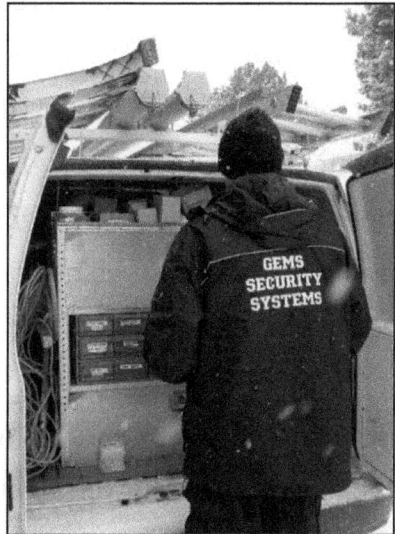

Our technical staff are selected and hired for their experience and competence in the field. They are encouraged to maintain an open line of communication with office management, mainly for status updates on their service and installation assignments.

Gems' technical support staff are indispensable to the field technicians who, in their daily tasks, come across countless different pieces of equipment, systems, installations, and locations of power supplies or control panels - just to mention a few hidden devices. Sometimes they are faced with antiquated technology, with no schematics left behind from the original installers, and absolutely no availability of system codes, wiring diagrams or floor plans for reference.

Our technicians understand that if servicing a multitude of different systems were easy, anyone could do it. But, because each product has its own unique and sometimes intricate set-up, it takes a real professional to troubleshoot, understand, and unravel what went wrong. This can sometimes be a long and tedious process. Open lines of communication with tech support are an essential source to filter through ideas that at times get clouded with the unknown or the not so obvious.

Know what you sell

Prior to selling a product to your customer, it is important to make sure that you, your technicians, and your sales staff understand the product you are selling, and know how to service it. Trying to obtain any project by promoting inexpensive and sub-standard equipment that may or may not last through the warranty period is irresponsible and does not make you an expert, or a serious security provider. Some providers sell monitored alarm systems to gain residual income, but in fact, these systems are only connected to answering machines in the installers' basements. This is the sign of a low-end security provider who will probably not last very long in the business.

Years ago I learned that being frugal saves money; but hindsight tells me that being meagre creates waste.

～～Words about Rose～～

"An NVR (network video recorder) manufacturer's representative kept pushing my sales staff to postpone one meeting after another for a product demonstration with our customer. In the meanwhile, the customer was getting very annoyed and I sensed we would risk losing him if we did not maintain his belief in our product for much longer.

This representative's attitude was just enough to trigger my less than congenial telephone conversations, and with some firmness I told him that I was no longer subjecting my customer to his unprofessional skirmishes.

A meeting was promptly set for the next day; the product demo was a real success, and we managed to retain the customer.

After the meeting, my sales staff returned to our office and told me Michael commented that if he had known he would be dealing with people like me, he would have chosen a different industry."

~~~~~End~~~~~

Prospecting

How do you find your customers?

You need top notch professional and communications skills when you are prospecting for customers. Remember to keep your personal opinions on a very short leash, and avoid engaging in discussions of a political, religious or personal nature with the prospect – or indeed with any customer for that matter!

Always be cautious and do not over-talk in an effort to capture your prospect's attention; this could backfire, and your potential customer might lose interest. You could have talked yourself right out of a sale.

Admittedly, cold calling is essential, but it is difficult and time-consuming. You need to measure the prospect's interest, their need for the product/service, and then deliver your pitch to the financial decision-makers.

In fact, listening is just as important as talking in almost any circumstance. You must be a people person and establish good rapport with both your suppliers and customers. Much of this is done by listening.

"If" never comes

Beware of the sales staff who practices a lot of *"Ifs"* and "When I was working for ... ." Recognize that this person is living in the past, believes in the unknown, and has a serious disconnect with the facts. This type of person is definitely a problematic investment.

<p align="center">~~~Story~~~</p>

"One of my employees was falling into a painfully slow and mundane routine and when he was asked what he was planning to do to accelerate his pace in order to deliver qualified leads, his answers always started with, *"If...."*

Each time, he delivered responses such as, *"If* I can reach this operations manager at this company, we can get some work"... *"If* I get a call back from this person at that cold storage place we may have an opportunity to quote"... *"If* this property manager returns my call soon, I may be able to get an appointment".

I made numerous attempts to re-educate his thinking but had no success. As days turned into weeks, and weeks turned into months, his performance remained the same: "*If*", "*If*", and "*If*".

One day I decided that a blunt and direct approach would be more successful so, when he started delivering the daily verbal report of his calls by saying "*If,*" and "*If*", I interrupted him and asked him to listen to me: "*If* my grandmother had b...s, she would have been my grandfather." Then I asked him what he thought of that reality.

That seemed to shock him into action and, from then on he greatly improved his performance and understood that "*If*" does not present facts and it is hard to get any results with an unknown or a hopeful abstract thought."

Rose's Insight: *Replacing the non-performers such as these will most likely always earn you a very descriptive and colourful name. You should try to ignore the name-calling, even though they reach you as darts with a sting. You need to stay the course and keep looking at the bigger picture.*

~~End~~

Explain, Educate, and Assure

To be a serious player in this industry, you must determine what the market needs, believe in your company's ability to deliver on those needs, and know how to take a project from start to finish. Staying current with any industry changes and being aware of details such as new products on the market, will help you to remain ahead of the game.

Once you have determined your customer's needs, you will distinguish yourself from lower-end security providers in a number of ways:

- Explain the benefits and warranties of the product you represent

- Educate customers about your business ethics

- Assure them that your company is up-to-date with labour policies, and

- Be ready to provide proof of documentation if and when it is required.

In short, mean what you say and deliver what you offered, and above all, never promise what you cannot deliver. Let your past and ongoing performance be proof of your company's abilities and your guiding force to future projects.

100% Professionalism in all things is non-negotiable!

(One of our installers working on a cctv system)

At Gems Security we will not consider installing video surveillance and access control systems on the cheap just in order to meet our competitor's price. Neither do we leave wiring unsecured or exposed, as it is an invitation for vandals to compromise the system. This is not an installation practice my company will entertain.

No matter how difficult the job, systems installers need to establish credibility with the customers by assuring them that they will not leave the site until the project is completed, tested, and they, the customers, have been trained how to use the equipment.

This is why in your security business, you must practice workmanship that is second to none, keep open communication with the customer, and keep detailed records of the work you have completed. When your installers are wearing your uniform to do their job, they are representing you, and they must treat the customer's premises with the utmost respect. They should complete the job as efficiently as possible and, when it is complete, leave the premises clean and in order.

Deviation from plans

Sometimes, without your permission, an employee or a supplier tries to change the plan that is already in place and accepted by your customer. For example, some specific items may not be in stock and your supplier wants to push a different product that does not meet the pre-sold specifications, just so he can make his inventory look good. Or your installer claims that the weather looks too threatening to proceed with the installation. Or sometimes even your own service technician does not want to go to the scheduled site at the end of the day in case he gets stuck in too much rush hour traffic.

None of these situations would meet your uncompromising quality of service that sets you and your company above the rest.

Unfinished business.

At Gems Security, we have at times been requested to take over projects that were left incomplete by other contractors. We also accept projects and systems that need service when the original contractor cannot be found and, as well, we take over and monitor security systems for customers who do not get a timely response from the original contractor when their alarm triggers.

These customers are left hanging, so our service department takes on those critical roles, while keeping an open dialogue with the customers, so as to get the specifications that may or may not have been left behind by the last company. If the technicians cannot get there as promised for any reason, the Service Department ensures that the customer knows the situation, and immediately offers an alternative solution, such as proposing the first appointment on the following day.

At the same time, we make it a point never to make a customer feel foolish for having made a bad choice with previous contractors. And we would never be critical of the competition in the customer's presence. We also make it a practice to offer something extra to add value to our service. For example, customers receive parking enforcement, a free camera, a general security audit, or even a free alarm monitoring service from time-to-time.

I have found that assuming these services brings goodwill in abundance, and I would advise that you definitely adopt that approach in your own business.

Ongoing Delivery of Service

If you are developing a service company and you have staff to undertake the daily operations, it is important to realize that even if you excel in administration and/or sales, there are very many other areas that need to be covered appropriately, and which you need to staff with knowledgeable people. If a customer has a service problem, you cannot pretend to resolve the issue by taking short cuts; you will only provide temporary respite until you need to face the inevitable, and do the job properly – which you might as well have done in the first place.

Because of the nature of the security industry, your service must be delivered with speed and the utmost efficiency. There is no way that you can set up a 9:00am – 5:00pm working schedule like many other industries and offices. Emergencies can hit 24/7 and you must arrange for staff and equipment to be available to respond at any time of the day or night without too much delay. For example, weather storms can disrupt the function of access controls and camera systems, causing major stress and huge security concerns for industrial and commercial sites.

Your company must have enough stock on hand and staff ready to service your customers on short notice in order to minimize damage to premises and people. Your main concern is to reassure customers of your company's ability to make their situation your security priority. At Gems' premises, we keep some equipment on hand for emergencies to meet just the scenarios described above. The equipment for regularly booked installations is ordered as needed from our suppliers.

Sabotage

~~~Story~~~

"An attempt at sabotage came from my IT (Information Technology) technician. This shy individual was employed by my company for a period of two years and in that time he became familiar with several of my customers, as well as the equipment we installed and serviced. He was a talented middle-aged man with a lot of technical knowledge and was proud of himself when he found solutions to obscure technical problems that were not just a simple and quick fix that anyone would know.

Unfortunately, he did not seem to be aware of the clock, and quite often did not complete his assignments in a timely fashion. His work ethics demonstrated two speeds: slow and stop.

Eventually we parted company and even though he was bound by a non-competitive and confidentiality clause, he left the company and took our new network codes with him, leaving us to fend for ourselves if the network system were to become problematic.

As he had anticipated, the network system required service and he made himself scarce and unreachable. After numerous failed attempts to communicate with him in order to retrieve the pass codes he had set-up, we sent him a registered letter to advise him that he was in possession of stolen intellectual property and that we would not hesitate to pursue the matter further if he did not release them to us (the owners) immediately.

He quickly complied."

Rose's Insight: *You must deal with each issue as it happens and find solutions that match the individual problems.*

~~~End~~~

The phony entrepreneur

~~~The Story Continues~~~

"Soon after the pass code matter was settled, some of my customers informed us that this individual had approached them to try and promote his own company. He offered to supply them with cameras, digital video recorders (DVRs) and network video recorders (NVRs).

Once more we wrote to him reminding him that he was in contravention of his agreement, and asked him to cease and desist immediately or face legal consequences.

Again he was set straight."

Rose's Insight: *The lesson from these experiences is that many people are under the delusion that being in business equals easy money. They believe that they can do really well with little investment, and so they attempt to do business with nothing. This is a big mistake.*

~~~End~~~

A Better Way - working up through the ranks.

Quite like all the staff, both my Executive Account Manager, Jason, and my Business Development Manager, Jim, carry all kinds of responsibility in their jobs and they work with both Gems and Gemstar. They both started with Gemstar as floating security guards, going where they were needed, and they worked their way up through the ranks. They each worked as static guards, patrol officers, alarm response officers, dispatchers and mobile supervisors. Their mandate now is to develop new business while maintaining good rapport with the existing customers. They also interact with suppliers and keep on top of any new product developments and project installations.

They are based in the office and each spends some planning time with me every morning, informing me of progress in the negotiations with new prospects and discussing their agenda for the day.

Rose Catalano

Jason has been with us since the inception of Gemstar Security and has now become my right hand man in the overall operation of Gems Security. His dedication to the company is unquestionable and he is never too proud to say that he has a lot to learn about the running of a security company.

Jim remembers early on sharing his goal with HR, stating that he wanted to make his career here, and help to build this company. He has now been with us for over 10 years and he definitely contributes to the daily synergy. He tells us how much he enjoys working here, and he considers that his "days are fun as opposed to work".

Gemstar Security Service

(One of the special events that our staff enjoyed was to provide the security for the Australian soft rock group 'Air Supply', when they performed in Toronto. Here they are on the job with the group members!)

As with Gems, our Gemstar staff are chosen and trained to perform their duties exceptionally. Our company's success rests upon capable employees who understand our company model and can deliver our services effectively and with positive energy. These people are our ambassadors out there in front of the public.

HR and the value of a well-written memo

Human Resources Managers must be knowledgeable about writing memos appropriately, especially regarding disciplinary procedures. They and other managers must know how to avoid writing memos that will encourage the employee to be defensive.

You must train your supervising staff to manage according to facts and not opinions. When opinions are freely permitted, the facts get lost, and it makes room for misunderstandings, minimizes the matter at hand, and could perhaps encourage gossip.

(Keeping up the records)

You should always record full and accurate employee documentation, especially if it is of an evaluative nature, and you should store it under lock and key for safety. Never discuss one employee's file with another. Curious employees may not be trustworthy, and when the chips are down, those prying employees could turn out to be your worst enemies as they will be quick to disclose what they know or heard about your company's affairs.

There is no question that confidentiality applies to everyone, with no exception, from upper management down, and all the way back up again!

A different staff situation

By now, you are beginning to understand some of the absurd staff issues that I am called upon to deal with. Here are a couple more.

~~~Story~~~

"Two employees constantly reported for work smelling very badly. Persistent body odour was the order of the day for them, and other employees refused to work near them. Something needed to be done. So HR addressed the situation with one person, and the mobile supervisor talked to the second person. Both employees were offered solutions to correct their BO, but neither one of them received this information well and both were in denial and resentment.

Mobile officers continued to get complaints about the severe smell from the one employee and went as far as buying antiperspirant and soap for him, hoping he would deal with the offensive odour and make it possible for others to work in the same room. The other employee temporarily improved the problem, but was soon back to his usual unpleasant condition.

The worst odour offender was finally released as the BO was insufferable and incessant, and the one who temporarily remedied his condition remains as work in progress. Other than the 'aroma', he is a productive employee."

~~~End~~~

And this one.

~~~Story~~~

"Another time, one of our installers was working in a residential dwelling, and he claimed to be having gastro intestinal issues. Thinking he needed to pass gas, he actually defecated in his pants right in front of the customer.

Needless to say he was sent home and a different installer had to complete the project. We were left with a customer who was not very pleased."

Rose's Insight: *When you have a business with hundreds of staff coming from all backgrounds and upbringings, you must be prepared to deal with any problems that come your way no matter how uncomfortable you might feel about it. At the same time, you must always be considerate of your employees' well-being.*

~~~End~~~

Regulations

The security business in Ontario is regulated by the Private Security and Investigative Services Act, 2005 (PSISA), which governs the licensing and behaviour of security guards and their employers. This process, mandated by the Ministry of Community Safety and Correctional Services in Ontario in order for guards to obtain licenses, is a costly training and testing program.

Guard Training

Training for guards is mandated and essential, and they must obtain their licenses before being hired. To be licensed, all guards are required to complete a forty-hour course which includes First Aid and CPR training, after which they must pass a written and oral test on security best practices. Once they clear the first test, they apply for a written test with the Ministry of Community Safety and Correctional Services, and once they pass that test, they apply for a license. The license is renewed annually, as long as it has not expired. Should it

Rose Catalano

be past the expiry date, the guard is obliged to repeat the whole process over again. All jurisdictions have similar requirements, though the specific regulations vary from location to location.

The Act is an in-depth synopsis of the role, procedures, behaviour, and other required knowledge for licensed guards and you cannot be employed as a security guard in Ontario if you do not obtain the required license. Following is an excerpt from the PSIS Act:

"Licensing Requirements (subsection 10(1) of the PSISA)

In order to be eligible for a security guard license, all individuals must:

- Have completed the required training and/or testing.

- Be at least 18 years old.

- Possess a clean criminal record, according to the Clean Criminal Record Regulation.

- Be legally entitled to work in Canada.

  People who apply for a security guard license will be required to show proof that they meet all of these requirements. If they are not eligible for a security guard license, their application will not be processed."

92

The procedure is such that the individual pays fees and completes paperwork at every stage: to apply and participate in the forty hour in-class training session, to schedule and take the Ministry's test, and then yet another hurdle of paper work, and more expense to apply for the license – that is, if the individual passes the test.

Supplementary training must be delivered by security companies concerning each site that the guard is sent to. Obviously all sites are different depending upon the type of premises and the location in the city.

Further security roles

Additional and different levels of security training should be accessible to those individuals who possess obvious ambition and an ability to offer more, and those who demonstrate the competence to perform these advanced duties. Certain soft tasks that are now assigned to police officers could well be performed by trained security personnel. Such roles as road construction watch, accompanying funeral processions, and assisting in monitoring speeding drivers could well fit into the portfolio of security training.

Request to the Ministry - Expanding Guards' Roles

I would gladly accept an invitation to engage in more dialogue with the officials who are responsible to design the development of the security industry standards. I believe that the private sector, if they were given the opportunity, could offer major help in providing specially-trained officers to fill in for those non crime-fighting assignments. Police officers would then have more time available for other roles and to make an impact on the safety of their communities.

The current practice of using police services for these soft roles is costing tax payers very high premiums and is leaving much of the population short of patrol police officers in areas with sensitive needs.

～～～Words about Rose～～～

"We often commission Jerry, a man of superior stature, demanding personality, and a no-nonsense approach to self-defence, to train our staff in arrest procedures and use of force. Unfortunately, on one occasion, Jerry did not provide the guards with the training certificates upon completion of the training as per our agreement, and on another two occasions he missed his scheduled appointments. This caused unwarranted disappointments and unnecessary inconvenience for the guards and for the scheduling manager.

I decided to explain to Jerry, in my own lingo, that in no way was this permissible as each of the guard's time was valuable and must be respected. If he valued the contract, his attitude and delivery of responsibilities needed immediate adjustment.

Apparently the tone of my voice struck a chord in this man and he commented to the operations manager that he was not afraid of much, but this little 5'2" woman made him feel quite inept."

~~~~~~~End~~~~~~~

Security Guard Pay Issues

In Ontario, a trained and licensed security guard will earn minimum or slightly above minimum wage, which is lower than average job earnings in our province. For that remuneration, they are required to be available to work different daily shifts, and be on call to work week-ends if and when required. The standards of pay have been set very low, and yet we expect the guards to be knowledgeable, pleasant, wise, capable of writing detailed reports, and be ready to respond to any event or situational escalation if the need arises.

Unfortunately, being a security guard is not the most inspiring avenue to pursue, unless the candidate is using the experience as a springboard for other careers. Consequently, staff turnover in the security guard area is constant, and it demands an extraordinary amount of time from Human Resources (HR) for that reason.

To be more realistic, the present standards must be reviewed and changed. I would argue that for the past many years neither the government nor the private sector has done enough to ensure a fair wage for security guards, and I believe it is critical for the Ministry to undertake serious consultation and involvement with the private sector in order to design a more affordable and accessible security program. What I see missing is a plain common-sense approach to providing security service. It appears that the dollar influences the whole process with little consideration for the individual.

The Healthcare industry, for example, is notorious for paying their guards minimum wage, while expecting them to be physically fit and ready to de-escalate issues when patients lose control. With all the responsibilities and expectations put on security guards, we certainly pay them less than those who mop the floors, or clean the rest rooms in hotels, hospitals, or condominiums. This is a deplorable situation, and must be changed.

Today, with revisions to the minimum wage standards, and continued efforts put forth by the security providers, we are offering our customers a higher level of service such as concierge duties, parking supervision, report preparation etc., all of which should lead to increased financial commitment on their part. Minimum wage revision will encourage the concierge, the patrol guard, and the static guards to value their jobs, improve their performances, and take pride in their chosen professions. I do not anticipate that the revolving door in the security guard industry will slow down any time soon, but I have hope that the gap will be minimized, thus giving breathing room to customers and suppliers alike.

Apart from the expense, a couple of issues affect our company management. One is when a guard completes the in-house training and becomes knowledgeable about site specific procedures, and he/she then immediately leaves us for another company. There is nothing I can do about that but search for a replacement guard and repeat the training process all over again.

A second issue is the time and cost involved for guards to train in the use of force, arrest procedures, self-defence and use of batons. We encourage the mobile guards and employees who work at challenging sites to refresh these skills at least twice a year. All this time cuts into their working hours in an already tightly-scheduled timetable and puts more demands on their financial situations. To alleviate this problem, our Operations Manager, Dave, is preparing to qualify in providing this tactical training and administering the physical testing at our premises. This will streamline the whole process for our employees and also for management. We trust it will expedite the time involved to arrange for these classes, and cut back on the expenses for the employees, as this training will be provided at no cost to them.

It is a win-win solution for everyone.

Why do people join the security industry?

Leonora is a guard who has been with Gemstar for ten years and works between a couple of shifts in the evening (5:00pm – 10:00pm) and overnight (11:00pm-5:00am). She can request her building, which would then determine her shift, and she usually gets what she asks for. Leonora is in a position to attend these shifts regularly and is also available for longer hours, which works for her. Her job is routine and she gets to know the residents, who become very comfortable with her. There are some people who worry about their personal safety, and she is able to reassure them that she is monitoring for intruders and keeping them safe.

Leonora observed that guards usually stay from five to ten years with Gemstar Security Service, and she has been there longer than most. This woman is content in her job, and appreciates that her bosses are pretty good at keeping the "family" of staff together "by asking us what we need". She once called me the "mother" of the company, like "a mom with all her kids". Leonora could have worked her way up into a higher position with the company, but she is happy with her current arrangement, and does not seem to have the desire to do so.

For the most part, people join this industry for a couple of reasons, money not being one of them. While some guards are quite happy to remain where they start, others work up through the company or, to my great pride, they use the experience as a foundation before moving to other related careers, such as the RCMP or Correctional Centres.

- Some want to venture into higher profile security work and this experience is a stepping-stone to other positions in the public service sector, such as police constables, prison guards, parking enforcement, private investigators and more.

- Others may have lost their jobs and have been unable to get something comparable to what they had. In order to meet their existing financial commitments, they now work two lower paying jobs, one of which is security.

- Some imprudently join the industry specifically to work only on construction sites. They think they will sit at the site, read the paper, and catch up on some sleep. The realization that they actually need to be a productive member of the team hits them hard, and they soon become unemployed again.

• Then we have those who take their responsibilities seriously, work for the company's best interests, and learn as much as they can in order to be an asset for Gemstar.

• In time their efforts are recognized and appreciated and they move on to supervisory positions or administrative duties.

(This group of guards had just completed an assignment at a Beer Fest in a city north of Toronto)

Cost of Doing Business

When you run any business, there are many expenses – most are obvious and expected, such as your office and utility expenses, your payroll, capital outlay etc., but others are hidden and unexpected, such as new industry regulatory upgrades, legal fees to deal with tax issues, and collection fees to retrieve money that is owing to you.

You could also consider other ways of managing your funds, such as the occasional joint venture offer if one is presented to you. But make sure to investigate thoroughly and consider it seriously.

~~~Story~~~

"John owned and operated a private investigation agency with assignments spread through Washington DC, the Middle East, and Ontario. In the late 1990s his business started to slow down, and he was required to put his world-wide expansion plans temporarily on hold while he checked out other options. He began to look for other areas in the security business where he could add to his profile.

I received word that he wanted to meet with me to discuss a possible joint venture, so I took two of my staff members and met John and his assistant in his office. My companions and I were curious, but at the same time skeptical, about the intent of this meeting. We listened carefully to his speech, and took notes for reference in case of further discussions in the near future. When the three-hour meeting was over, however, we exchanged cordialities, and I told him that at this time his proposal was cold. If there were any changes, I would advise him in the next few days.

This man had taken a cavalier attitude with us, and told us that he possessed a wealth of practical private security investigation experience, and had established all the right contacts to expand his operation into Florida and Western Ontario.

Nevertheless, he was missing the Agency License to operate a security guard company, and the technical staff to operate the electronic equipment side. This is where he thought my company would come in handy, and he offered to provide contact names to help us expand, while he and his assistant would hold the operational control.

My responsibility would be to provide all start-up costs, including insurance coverage. As we know, coverage outside of Ontario would not be cheap, or even possible, especially if we were looking at the possibility of staff relocation. Simply put, it was not a proposal I could consider, even if having an operation in Florida sounded enticing. There was a distinct possibility, even a strong probability, of it being a total disaster.

John's proposal was not entertained. He was obviously disappointed, and labeled me a "rare commodity" in the industry, presumably for standing my ground against his 'inviting' stories.

Shortly after, John started a technical division on his own and approached two of my staff members to join him with get-rich-quick promises. They both took the bait and accepted the enticement. One of the employees who left contacted me four months later and begged for his job back. John's electronic division had shut down, and he has never spoken to me since."

Rose's Insight: *The moral of this story is that you would be well-advised to stay your own course and not be tempted to overstretch or you may risk hurting both yourself and your pocket book.*

∾∾End∾∾

Though I have never actually seen a hard line between reality and fantasy, I can tell you that too much fantasy will make that imaginary line very blurry.

Even so, I occasionally become overwhelmed with the constant costs of doing business, especially with the frequency of training the guards and/or technicians who then immediately leave my employ for perceived better opportunities elsewhere.

But then the alarm bells go off, the lights come on, and I connect the dots and quickly acknowledge that Gems and Gemstar are not only about me. So I pull myself together and it is business as usual; doubt and self-pity are denied access into my office.

How you treat your staff

As a company owner, you must take your responsibilities seriously and lead by example. You should create an atmosphere of equality among your staff and, most importantly, remember to show appreciation for their efforts. Your employees are your front line workers and they represent you and your company in the field. If your customers consider the guards, your installers, or your technicians incompetent, this reflects on you and therefore also on your company.

You cannot do without them; they are your ambassadors, so treat them fairly and equitably and, above all, communicate with them. For example, it is not advisable to put guards on a site without them having specific knowledge of site requirements. This information creates a feeling of competence and without it, there could be a potential for serious consequences for the customer, your company, and the guard.

You also need to be confident in the performance of your staff, both in protection of property, and installation and maintenance of systems.

Drinking on the job

Story

"An employee of several years as installer and service technician knew his job well and, for the most part, performed it well. Eventually, though, he started drinking after working hours – at first it was occasionally, and then it became more frequent. Soon he started to complain that he was short of cash and could not afford to take his two little girls to the dentist. Meanwhile it was reported to me that he had now started drinking in the office parking lot as soon as he brought the truck back at the end of the day. Then shortly afterwards, he started missing days from work, claiming he was sick, and distraught because he could not look after his little girls properly.

I offered to give him $5,000 to take care of the family and I requested that he pay the company back in installments when he was in a better financial position. I also strongly suggested that he get himself together and stay on the right track.

He appreciated my help and said that the loan would really help out, but two weeks later he quit his job, the money that my company loaned him was spent, and the little girls never made it to the dentist or to McDonalds for lunch as he had promised them. He asked Human Resources (HR) to falsify the Record of Employment (ROE) by saying he was laid off, so he could collect employment insurance benefits. We refused and processed the ROE as it should be done.

This man totally misjudged my earlier kindness, and filed a report against my company stating that I had paid him $5,000 without making the proper tax deductions. Unfortunately for me and my company, since I had deemed this a personal loan given in trust, I did not draw up or maintain any documentation."

Rose's Insight: *Since this incident, I have taken great care never to allow this type of error in judgment to get past me again. Now I always record every transaction in detail, no matter what the size of the amount or the nature of the event.*

<div align="center">~~~End~~~</div>

Preparation for Emergencies

(Concierge taking notes for the records)

Never assume any site or project responsibilities will be easily managed by your field staff alone. You or your management staff need to be prepared for emergencies and your staff should be trained in every detail. You must provide complete planning to cover every eventuality you can think of based on the different premises and their amenities, and then be ready to respond immediately in the event there is an escalation on site.

A tragic event

~~~Story~~~

"Recently, a horrible accident occurred at one of our sites – a little girl drowned in the swimming pool. A condominium board member, who was onsite at the time, went to the security desk to view the video and witnessed how our site guard, the site supervisor and mobile supervisors jumped into action and assisted the public response teams (police, ambulance, fire) without confusion or delay.

Our team kept the media at a distance and avoided discussions with other tenants in an effort to minimize panic and confusion. Although the situation was extraordinarily difficult and emotional, the performance of our staff was exemplary and by the book.

After a few days, this board member requested to meet with top management from my company because she was not happy with how my staff handled themselves during this tragic accident. Feeling confident that my staff had indeed exercised the correct procedures, and without any reservation that we had come up short in our dealings with the site and tenants, my operations manager and I attended the meeting.

This board member was accompanied by two other members of the board, who kept mostly silent. She yelled at us, swore, made constant ridiculous threats, and most of all lied about the actual events that took place. We know this because the cameras told a different story. She falsely accused my staff of not being trained, being confused and misguided. She accused my upper management staff of being careless and unprofessional, and told us, among other things, that our contract was put on notice.

At this time I deemed her false allegations not worth dignifying with an answer so we remained calm, made sure our notes reflected the events, and sent this information to the rest of their Board of Directors, who made sure that our reputation prevailed. In my assessment a person in her state of mind may be in need of serious medication; however, I was not licensed to prescribe Prozac or any other helpful medication!

The property manager was embarrassed at what she had witnessed. This woman, who thought that being a board member of a condo corporation somehow made her judge and executioner of any contractor, was told by other board members that she was out-of-line and bullying contractors was not a prerequisite to serve on their board.

Our contract was not in jeopardy.

Recently we heard that this woman's aura has faded both at the condo and at her place of work. Her self-proclaimed inportance does not work for her any longer. Perhaps she is lonely!"

Rose's Insight: *To retain the upper hand in situations like this, do not descend to the level of those who accuse you. Stay calm, record all details meticulously, and send your notes to the appropriate body, which will make the final decision.*

Integrity is a rewarding quality.

~~~End~~~

A guard on a crusade

It is not only the people in so-called positions of authority who throw their weight about and try to intimidate others, it also happens in the ranks of the guards.

~~~Story~~~

"One of our long term and trusted employees – an Eastern European refugee who had been working for Gemstar at very challenging sites, was stranded in Germany while trying to go

114

back home to visit his family. Due to his previous international conditions, he was not granted passage to his country from Germany and was given three days to leave that country. He did not have enough cash to purchase another ticket for his trip back to Canada and in desperation he called our office for help. Gemstar Security wired him sufficient funds to bring him back to Canada.

Once he arrived back in Canada we reinstated him at his original assignment. Yet, within a few weeks of his return to work, his demeanor changed and he became increasingly unpredictable and difficult to work with. He started to push us, by making demands for unreasonable wage increases and requesting extra hours to boost his pay.

Thinking he was indispensable, this guard started to make threats about leaving the company, and when that didn't work, he had the audacity to approach our customer directly and told him that he was worth more than Gemstar was paying. He also claimed that he had information about the site that he would disclose unless his demands were met. This man told the customer that he was broke and had not had food for at least two days. The customer, out of courtesy and concern, loaned him some cash.

This loan proved to be a short term fix. Feeling self-assured
that this customer could be manipulated by fear and would
bow to his demands, the guard re-visited him and demanded
that he provide our company with a substantial rate increase
so that we would have no choice but to adjust his rate of pay
in turn.

When that scenario did not play out as he had hoped, he
began to cause damage to the property and then falsify the
reports by stating that he saw the superintendent of the
building purposely damage walls, doors, and windows.

This employee, who had been shown kindness from both the
company and the customer, had now become an actual
liability for both parties. His arrogant behaviour had no place
in our business and with the customer's cooperation, his file
backed up his unacceptable behaviour.

At this point, HR prepared his Record of Employment (ROE),
calculated the severance that was due to him as per the
Ontario Employment Standards Act, gave him the envelope
and sent him packing. Once he realized that the severance
package would not last forever and that he had overstepped
the mark, he offered an apology and asked for his job back,
whereupon reinstatement was flatly refused. Next, out of

desperation, he approached our customer to ask him to intervene and urge us to give him the job back.

It didn't happen. I suspect he eventually understood that it was not wise to assume that instigating fear would overcome his self-induced problem and still leave hope for reinstatement."

Rose's Insight: *Accepting or condoning such irresponsible behaviour from present or ex-employees is simply not acceptable in my business. This ungrateful man must have looked in the mirror only to see egg on his face!*

Self-respect and respect for others must be the trump card in any infrastructure.

~~~End~~~

Standards of Uniform

Guards

(A supervisor in uniform and at the ready!)

Each site where you have a guarding assignment is different. Be ready for anything by ensuring that the guards have been given appropriate written and verbal instructions, and they are aware of specifics and information about the site. They also require proper uniform, including the necessary accessories, such as duty belt, flash lights, bullet-proof vests, hand cuffs. In that way you, and they, are as prepared as possible for most eventualities. When there is a totally unexpected event, their good training immediately kicks in and takes over, and beyond that, your guards rely on intuition and their own speedy response.

Because the guards are required by law to wear a uniform, the company invests in the initial clothing cost, and the employee makes minimal payments back to Gemstar to cover these expenses. We also have an open door policy to discuss special arrangements with part-time employees and employees with extenuating circumstances.

Technicians

(Gems Security uniform)

Make sure that your technicians and guards wear clean and well-pressed uniforms and that their appearance is a credit to your company. A well-outfitted employee makes a positive company statement.

Selecting your staff

You must be a good judge of character and of personality traits to select appropriate staff to meet your standards and policies. But no matter how well you think you have chosen, you will find that many of your employees possess ingenious minds that will test your own decisions. It seems as if everyone comes with a problem and you must be able to think quickly, especially when your staff are reporting their activities or events to you, and telling you about everything that took place during the previous day/evening/night shifts – much of which could be either embellished or even diminished.

This industry is people-driven and you soon discover that you will face mindless, unfounded excuses as well as sad stories. When you are assessing issues, and making decisions about handing out disciplinary notices, you must train yourself to understand your employees' behaviour, thoughts, and methods of operation. This can sometimes be difficult as you unravel and sift through the rubbish that gets dished out to you at any given time.

From the collection of excuses I have heard

~~~*Excuses*~~~

"Employees do not show up for work, claiming that their grandmother suddenly died. A few months later they do it again, and then again, and again, until you remind them that the grandmother has now died about 6 times in the last 10 months. Quite often they answer "Ah!" and you hope they will remember the next time."

~~~*Excuse*~~~

"One employee actually called us half an hour before his shift to say that he could not come to work because he had forgotten his daughter was getting married that evening."

~~~*Excuses*~~~

"The best excuses and explanations come from the guards who are caught sleeping on the job. They never admit they were sound asleep and totally unaware of their surroundings; their explanation is always the same, "I was only resting my eyes.""

~~~*Excuse*~~~

"Don't be surprised to hear that an employee will not be coming to work because the boyfriend or girlfriend broke their heart the night before. Scrambling to fill their shift on such short notice is apparently not their issue; it is someone else's problem."

And my own personal favourite:

~~~*Best excuse*~~~

"Another guard did not show up to the site, nor did he advise the office that he would be taking the night off. When we finally reached him and reminded him of his, and our, obligations to the customer, he said his wife had grounded him and had taken his car away so he had no transportation to get to work."

~~~*End*~~~

Will a mediocre performance improve?

You must also be able to recognize the weak performer, and identify if this employee is actually trainable to the extent that he will attain your company's standards. Or will he or she simply remain average? Mediocrity and idleness should have no place in this fast-paced and very competitive industry.

You are looking for top quality actions from your staff, and you will find that habitual minimal performers will always give you minimal results. If you maintain these less than standard employees for too long in your organization, they will simply become a drain on your resources. Replacing them, however, will most likely poke holes in your pocket and clutter your day. Simply stay the course, and keep your eye on the bigger picture.

Everyone's best performance pays the bills, and your staff's wages. You must keep the well-being of all your employees in mind without being discriminatory, judgmental, or unfair to anyone. And when you observe emergent and increasing ability, then is the time to promote that person. Remember, though, that promotion does not always reflect current seniority. You promote the high performer, the person who has proven that they will do the job best.

Expansion and moving

As my company progressed and developed, so did our requirements for more space. We needed larger premises, which would fit our current growth, and yet leave room for expansion in the future. I began an area search for my new offices. We needed to find a new location with enough space and, at the same time, we had to plan the move so that there was minimal disruption to the running of the business.

This required some strategic planning, and choosing a new location was difficult. Because of our unique business requirements, we needed easy access to highways and bus routes, and we needed to take into account new travel time

for our current employees. All that and figuring out the costs of moving almost jammed my calculator!

In addition to the above considerations, I had to think about whether to purchase or lease. I thought about how much space I really needed, and how long that space would last for us. I did not want to over-expand, yet I wanted to have enough space for the next five to ten years of growth. How do you truly forecast what space a service company such as mine would require in that time? It was very difficult.

Finally, I made a decision and purchased a unit in an industrial complex north of the city that seemed to be a prime location, with the travel advantages I was seeking for ease of operation. It suited our needs well and the move was accomplished.

Outgrowing the Expansion

After only six years at this location, however, I found that the number of vehicles my company operated far outnumbered the parking spots available to me. This was something

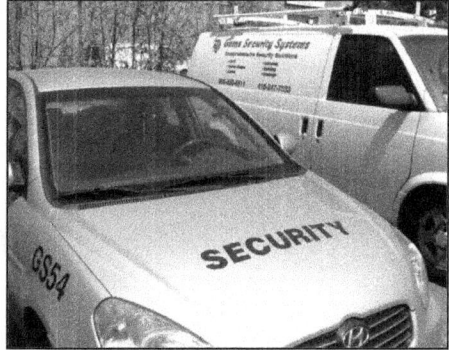

I had not anticipated and certainly had failed to forecast when planning for the move.

Fortunately, my property neighbours and the board of directors were not serious sticklers for strict rules, and they willingly accommodated my parking needs.

This exercise taught me that even though my move turned out to be imperfectly planned, a well thought out and fairly-negotiated tactic served my new purpose and enabled me to move forward.

Serving on the Board of Directors

As the years passed in my new location, and I developed friendships with neighbouring business owners, I began to take an interest in the welfare and operation of this industrial complex that housed my business. So, along with two other

Rose Catalano

very qualified members, I offered my services on the Board of Directors, and I was elected to serve on the board for a period of three years - which then turned into twelve.

This experience was invaluable for me. I learned a lot about condominium corporation rules and regulations, and how they apply to business owners. My biggest role was to scrutinize all payments and ensure that expenses were justified. We monitored that common areas were used as intended, and that the property management kept appropriate and complete data files, as well as applying the rules equally and fairly for every owner.

I consider myself fortunate to have had the privilege to serve on the board for so long and, though I no longer serve, the experience made me much wiser about industrial condominium financial structures, expenditures, structural upgrades and, as a side-benefit, harmony in decision making.

Giving back to the community

Children's party

Lest you think that my life consists completely of having to solve problems and dealing with troublesome staff and customers, it does not. There are many occasions where we enjoy humour and happiness. For example, a few years ago at Christmas time, Gemstar and Gems inaugurated what has become an annual tradition. We invite customers and suppliers, and their families, to Christmas celebration parties, where they enjoy a multi-course meal, with entertainment, and door prizes. Our only request of them is that guests bring along an unwrapped gift to be donated to Sick Children's Hospital and the Ronald McDonald house.

(The prize table at one of our Christmas celebration parties.)

The office staff all participate in organizing the event, held at a banquet hall, for which we pick up the tab. The staff take the initiative and each year, they inquire what the children need most. They have discovered that young teens at Ronald McDonald House, whose parents cannot stay with them due to financial or other reasons, appreciate telephone calling cards so they can contact their loved ones at Christmas time. Make-up kits for the girls, and board games are among some of the other favourite gifts.

Every guest who has attended is extremely generous with their gifts, and in the past, many families have brought more than the one toy that we request. It is seriously heartwarming, and everyone has lots of fun. Some years we have even collected so many presents that our staff have had to make several trips to pick up all the donations.

Delivering this abundance of goods to the recipients is equally rewarding, and to think about the smiles that we put on these children's faces at this very special time of year is the most gratifying act of kindness we could perform.

Student Scholarships

At Gemstar Security, we believe strongly in youth education, and we searched for a worthwhile cause that was related to our business.

(This shield was presented to Gemstar Security by NASSLEO in appreciation of our relationship with the Association.)

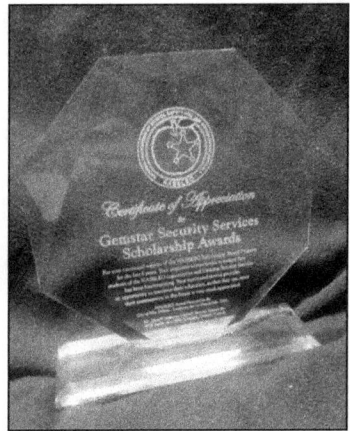

The National Association of School Safety and Law Enforcement Officials (NASSLEO) trains guards and, in an effort to recruit and place appropriate young people, the Association annually hands out scholarships to students in North America.

NASSLEO has been a good match for Gemstar, and we have donated scholarships for the past eight years. Graduates from High School, or students attending College or University may qualify for the scholarships. As well as attaining satisfactory marks, they must also show a positive contribution to their community. The money awarded to the students helps them with some of their expenses such as meal plans and books.

In search of superlative product

The R and D project

I have always been intrigued with different product applications and performance and, about ten years ago, I was looking for a superior paging system that could be utilized in airports or prisons. I wanted a product that excelled in quality and was clearly audible. I eventually discovered such Public Address (PA) equipment being manufactured in Munich, Germany. Unfortunately, this application had not yet reached Canada.

With the assistance of the Research and Development Department of the Federal Government, Gems Security contacted the Klotz Digital AG Company in Germany and after many conversation with Mr. Claus Wortmann, VP Worldwide Sales and Marketing, I was convinced that I wanted to explore this avenue. The possibility that my company could be innovative enough to study this product to discover if it was in fact one of the best in the market, encouraged me to continue to organize just the right team members who were qualified to assist me in this venture.

After many months of project planning and equipment investigation, our venture was approved by the Government, and we received the green light to proceed. With the guidance of the Canadian Consulate in Germany, we made our travel arrangements with clearance to visit active systems in Munich and Liechtenstein.

In Munich, we were met by several officials from Klotz Digital and over several days we had many conversations regarding the products and their distribution. Then came the highlight of the trip; we had received our airport clearance. So, accompanied by two police cars with flashing lights, one in front and one behind our car, we were escorted to the brain of the airport security system. We felt like VIPs, important officials, but in reality our escorts were simply making sure that we went where we were supposed to go, and nowhere else!

We saw the panel locations, and were given a sophisticated introduction and visual tour of their system in action. What a thrill it was! The installation was impeccable, and the audibility was second to none. We were awestruck and at a loss for words to describe that system.

After that experience, we were accompanied to Liechtenstein by Claus's assistant, where we were privileged to see yet another of their superior products in action. The complexity and product performance were truly outstanding.

Rose's Perception: *This was a most exhilarating experience for me and my team, and it reminded us that we need to be vigilant and open minded in this ever-evolving industry. New products come along with such speed and regularity that learning about them is almost a daily requirement – and it does not only apply to alarm systems. Regardless of where you are in your business continuum, augmentation and expansion should be close friends.*

A Word to the Ministry on abuse of the system.

We are a population of many diverse backgrounds and cultures, and we all have one thing in common: we desire safety and security for ourselves, our families, and our premises. I strongly believe that security providers must continue to work with the appropriate Ministry authorities to define other areas that would benefit from the participation and increased training of private security services.

Over the years, I have had a lot of experience with the government and the various Acts and Regulations that apply to security services and I have some thoughts about ways that the government could improve their approach.

A strong suggestion, one that I am convinced would curb abuse in the system, would be to suggest that the Ministry of Safety and Correctional Services has an open door policy to encourage and allow security providers to confidentially report offences committed by licensed security guards. These offences could include drug use, repeated falsification of incident reports, and guards commonly considered to be a menace or risk to others. These criminals are known to go from one security job to another, and no one stops this abuse of the system, because currently there is no vehicle to convey the details.

I am personally aware of licensed guards committing such offences.

<p align="center">~~~Story~~~</p>

"We had a guard assigned to do security patrols at a condominium complex, and we were notified by two board members that they suspected him of slashing people's tires when he didn't get his own way. The board of directors were so afraid of him that they asked us to reassign him away from their site.

The end result is that in order to avoid compromising your customers' contracts, this individual is simply dismissed from your employ (necessarily with pay), and he or she then moves on to some other unsuspecting victim in the system and repeats the same behavior with his next security provider and customer placement.

These security guards, licensed yet guilty, now develop the notion that they are entitled to move from property to property, and continue with the same inappropriate behavior, all the while knowing that the companies are powerless to do anything about it. This ace that only serves as a destructive habit should be removed from that deck of cards."

Rose's Insight: *It is common knowledge in the business, and somewhat disconcerting, that the present system does not offer an avenue worth pursuing when you have strong suspicions about a shameless security guard such as this. I would like to see the Ministry be more open to accepting the companies' concerns, and initiating a review system whereby companies are heard in cases such as these, and they know that justice will be served. Wouldn't this be a shot-in-the arm?*

<div align="center">~~~End~~~</div>

The following story also illustrates such abuse of the system, this time from an operations employee.

<div align="center">~~~Story~~~</div>

"We thought that we had found a competent and efficient woman to be our assistant office manager, because she performed well in both levels of her interview. In fact, what we had found was a manipulative and dishonest woman who was an experienced con-artist. She had provided us with false references and qualified for the position simply by preying on the unsuspecting.

Within three months, she had managed to show her true colours: she had frequent absenteeism, told lies about employee files, and spent an obscene number of hours advertising herself on the internet. Many of her work hours were also spent on the phone challenging the school officials about her son's homework, and suing her parents' insurance company because she slipped in their driveway while exiting from her vehicle ... and on and on it went.

When her poor performance was brought to her attention and she was put on extended probation, she claimed that her health and personal issues were causing her to under-perform in our stringent environment. She quickly brought in a note from a doctor claiming mental stress and saying that she needed to be on short term leave. We granted her a short leave and, in the meantime, due to economic turmoil, her position became redundant.

We eventually learned that she had skillfully mastered a devious plan that she would stay on a job approximately four to six months, and then devise a scheme that would most certainly get her fired or suspended. If she were not fired, she would plead sickness long enough for an employer to find a replacement for her position. And then she would refuse to accept a comparable position offered to her upon her return, claim wrongful dismissal, and sue for $2,500.

Because this amount would be considered negligible or not worthy of legal consideration by most companies, she had always come up the winner and easily pocketed the unearned cash. This time, however, her master plan didn't work. She had provoked an employer – me - who appreciates a good day's work and who detests those who have a total indifference to the valued of a dollar. In fact, her plan would cost her money as she had outsmarted herself with this game and now needed to consult with an expert.

I defended the claim and this process proved to be an unusually difficult and long ordeal for her. She eventually withdrew during mediation."

Rose's Insight: *I felt proud of my decision to challenge her claim and felt that the money and time I spent were well worth it. My unspoken message for her and others playing the same tricks was, "A thief will not always be successful to freely take from his neighbour and never face retribution." This disgraceful freeloader was an embarrassment to those of us who actually work to make a living.*

~~~End~~~

Some things to remember when you are considering the security industry

To be a significant player in this business, there are many aspects for you to learn, know, and remember. I have gathered them here in a list for your review to see if you think you would be a good fit.

Here are a few points to think about:

- Determine what the market needs

- Believe in your company's ability to deliver on those needs

- Know how to take a project from start to finish

- Be a people person

- Have endless energy and drive

- Establish good rapport with your suppliers

- Be aware of new products on the market

- Stay current with any industry changes, and

- You must also be exceptionally detail-oriented.

Professionalism is a non-negotiable asset for my company and should not be taken for granted.

Regular Company Review

Throughout my many years in this security business I have made it a practice to regularly assess and think about my business, its progress, and the benefits both to me and my family, as well as my employees and their families, my customers, and my suppliers. Even when I believe that things are running smoothly, I regularly receive sudden wake-up calls reminding me I still need to be on my toes.

I share with you some of my thoughts and conclusions arising from these years of experience, and more things to consider if you are thinking about a business in the security industry.

Here are some important points worth considering and aspiring towards.

You must

- Be in control of your own agenda – you are the Chief Executive Officer (CEO) of your own business and the ultimate decision-maker. Whether you thrive or falter is up to you and when you have a strong team, your decisions will be made with their input.

- Build the fortitude to withstand and overcome the many daily challenges and business obstacles that come your way.

- Take pride that you have built a team that works not only *for* you, but *with* you.

- Make an affirmative statement by being one of the travelers on the journey to a world of constant technical and electronic change.

- Be an active explorer, not simply a distant observer, of a society in quest of safety and security for people and premises.

- Realize that a win-win comprehensive security program is truly attainable.

- Trust that level-headed Ministry authorities together with leaders from the private security sector, and guided by the legal experts, can make our communities safety and security havens respected by any tax payer.

Remember

- Your fiscal year-end results mirror your efforts and provide gratification for a job well done.

- There is no substitute for a sense of accomplishment.

- You will derive satisfaction in being able to give back to society through foundations such as National Association of School Safety and Law Enforcement Officials (NASSLEO), the Sick Children fund, Cancer Research Centre, Ronald McDonald House, Missing Children fund, and many other needy organizations.

- Enjoy the reward that you and your employees share and be proud of your vision and your accomplishments.

- Experience and relish those magical times when the dynamics of your company precede you. When you answer the phone and ask the caller where they heard about your company, it is music to your ears when they say they were referred by a satisfied customer. It is especially gratifying to me when the referral has come from a male in the business!

- Realize that your dream is an actual reality and it is your company that makes someone's day better because of you or your staff who were there to help.

Rose Catalano

- You meet and get to know the many special and
  interesting people who have shared the same journey as
  you – sometimes along the same rough terrain, but
  perhaps in a different industry.

Today...

Today, we at Gems and Gemstar are still in the same location, and we are a profitable organization. I employ a substantial number of full-time staff and several floaters and sub-contractors who fill in the part time and/or short-term assignments. The company has expanded its horizons, and now has a fleet of vehicles dedicated to servicing the schools of several Boards of Education, and many other industrial and commercial sectors.

Rose Catalano

(Almost) The Last Word

I still believe in the notion of "walk, don't run". Business is not a race to the finish line, but a journey of slow and steady growth. If you adopt an attitude of bravado and try to play uncertain business games, you risk a strong possibility of failure and loss. The uncertainties cannot be underestimated, thus I have chosen to be content with *a little bit of something,* which I believe is much better than *a whole lot of nothing.*

Since I first began all those years ago, I have learned a great deal about every aspect of this business, the people I manage, and others with whom I do business, and these years have by no means been all smooth sailing. I discovered early on that it requires total commitment, tolerance, a good grasp of financial management, good customer relations techniques, open communication lines with customers and staff, good disciplinary programs, and most important of all, continuous training coupled with awareness of the movement and growth of the security business and its applications.

My place in the Industry

I can certainly confirm that I have earned my place in the security arena through knowledge, serious hard work, and most definitely respect for my customers. I have learned to work with a sense of urgency, and I am always aware of economic shifts as soon as they happen. Any deviance from that path, and I know I risk losing my space in an instant, no matter how long I have been in the business.

Just as I have come a long way, so has the security business. Private security was first introduced in the mid-nineteenth century in Sweden by Philip Sorenson, and in the United States by Allan Pinkerton. In the relatively short time of 165 years, the American security industry has expanded massively to almost $350 billion, of which approximately $280 billion is attributed to private sector spending. A recent BBC report stated that since 2011, the UK security services industry has increased by approximately four percent, to current security sales of $4 billion in that country.

So, remember, if you are reading about my journey from anywhere in the world, look around, and you will see signs of the security industry everywhere. This means that for you, anything is possible - just like it was for me

I offer these experiences to you, the women of today, wherever you are located, and if you have any aptitude and interest at all in starting and running your own business, this security industry is at the same time satisfying and challenging. I have paved the way for you, and I strongly believe that if I can do it, so can you!

How about it ladies?

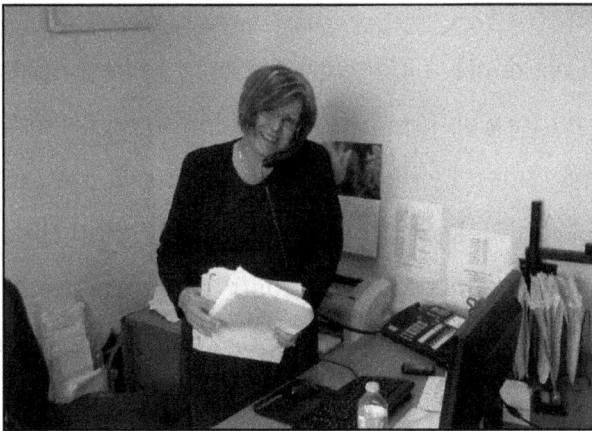

Rose Catalano
("My work is never done; I am multitasking in my office.")